A
NORTH
Cookbook

Rosa Mashiter
Illustrated by **Linda Smith**

Appletree Press

First published in 1996 by
The Appletree Press Ltd.
19-21 Alfred Street, Belfast BT2 8DL
Tel. +44 232 243074 Fax +44 232 246756
Copyright © 1996 The Appletree Press Ltd.
Printed in the U.A.E. All rights reserved.
No part of this publication may be reproduced or
transmitted in any form or by any means electronic or
mechanical,photocopying, recording or any information
and retrieval system, without permission in writing from
The Appletree Press Ltd.

A Little North Country Cookbook

A catalogue record for this book is available in
The British Library.

ISBN 0-86281-570-3

9 8 7 6 5 4 3 2 1

A Note on Measures
All spoon measurements are level rather
than heaped. Recipes are for four unless
otherwise indicated.

The North Country is often thought of, mistakenly, as a purely industrial region of England. Away from the cities are swathes of unspoilt landscape and breathtaking scenery. The cooking of the North Country is based on down-to-earth dishes, designed to satisfy the hearty appetites of hard working communities living in a bracing climate. Farmers raise cattle and sheep, providing top quality beef and lamb as well as plenty of milk for the North Country's famous cheeses. With sea to the East and West fish is plentiful, and battered fish and chips are a particularly popular dish in this region. Batters are very much a part of Northern cooking, with Yorkshire pudding an important feature on the lunch menu every week. The Northern cook is generally a good and keen baker and pies, biscuits and cakes are an important part of the culinary tradition. The North Country is a vast region and each part has its own distinct and proud traditions of good food.

Traditional North Country Breakfast

In the North of England a large, nourishing, hot breakfast is one of life's essentials. A bowl of steaming porridge, followed by a feast of bacon rashers, sausages, black pudding, fried bread, tomatoes and fried eggs with the yolks nice and runny so the fried bread can be swished in it.

If you find yourself in Northumberland you must make time to visit Craster to buy some kippers. Craster kippers are unique in their method of kippering based on the salmon kippering technique introduced to Craster in 1840. The fish is split down the back, salted, and smoked for a brief time to produce a light cure.

To jug kippers: this is one of the best ways to cook kippers. Put them head down in a tall stoneware or Pyrex jug, pour in boiling water to cover and leave 8-10 minutes. Drain and serve with a knob of butter or a poached egg on top.

To grill kippers: put the kippers skin side up under a hot grill, when the skin curls up the kippers are done.

Leek and Potato Soup

The local horticultural shows held annually in most Northumberland villages create fierce rivalry amongst the local population. In the weeks leading up to the show endless hours are spent both day and night nurturing the vegetables, especially leeks. Secrecy is paramount, and no competitor is allowed even a glimpse of the opposition. All must wait for the day of the show to see who has produced the largest and finest to win the much coveted first prize.

6 leeks
3 large potatoes
2 oz (50g) butter
2 ½ pints (1.5 litres) chicken stock
Salt and freshly ground black pepper
Finely chopped fresh parsley

Trim the leeks and stand upright in a jug of slightly salted cold water for about 30 minutes - this helps remove any grit and dirt inside the leeks. Cut into thin slices. Peel and dice the potatoes. Melt the butter in a heavy saucepan, add the leeks and potatoes, cook over a medium heat until lightly golden. Pour over the stock, bring to the boil, season with salt and black pepper and simmer for about 30-35 minutes until the vegetables are tender. Sprinkle with a little chopped parsley and serve.

Pan Fried Flukes

In the North Country, 'Flukes' are small fish found in the shallows of Morecambe Bay. They used to cost as little as threepence each but are a bit more expensive now. A really fresh fluke has far more flavour than plaice and cooked whole on the bone can be almost as good as sole.

1 oz (25g) butter
1 tbsp (15 ml) oil
4 fresh fluke, gutted
Seasoned flour
1 tbsp (15 ml) finely chopped fresh parsley
Wedges of lemon

Heat the butter and oil in a large frying pan. Coat the flukes in seasoned flour and add to the pan. Cook over a gentle to medium heat for 3-4 minutes then flip over and cook the other side. Scatter the parsley into the pan and shake well. Once cooked transfer to a warm serving dish and garnish with wedges of lemon.

Fish Cakes

Fleets from Humberside trawl the North Sea for white fish like cod, haddock, whiting and plaice, and every Northerner will tell you that the best fish and chips come from "up North".

1 lb white fish
8 oz (225g) peeled and boiled potatoes
1 egg
1 oz (25g) butter
Dash of anchovy essence
1 tbsp (15ml) finely chopped fresh parsley
Salt and freshly ground pepper
4 oz (100g) fresh white breadcrumbs
Oil for shallow frying

Makes 8

Poach the fish over a gentle heat for about 15 minutes. Drain and remove the skin and bones and flake the flesh into a bowl. Push the potatoes through a sieve. Separate the egg. Melt the butter in a pan, stir in the fish, potatoes, egg yolk, anchovy essence and parsley, seasoning generously with salt and black pepper then chill for an hour. Divide the mixture into about eight pieces, and with lightly floured hands shape into cakes. Whip the egg white and dip each cake into the egg white and then into the breadcrumbs, ensuring that they are thoroughly coated. Heat the oil in a large frying pan and cook the fish cakes for about 2-3 minutes each side until golden brown.

Pickled Lune Salmon

The salmon from the River Lune which runs into Morecambe Bay are believed to be the best in the North West.

2 lbs (900g) salmon fillets
1 small onion, peeled and roughly chopped
2 carrots, peeled and sliced
1 stick celery, chopped
½ pint (300ml) white wine vinegar
¼ pint (150ml) dry white wine
Bouquet garni
Salt and white pepper

Put the salmon fillets into a large shallow pan, or a fish kettle, add sufficient water to barely cover, and poach until just tender. Remove the salmon, reserving the cooking liquid. Put the liquid with the vegetables into a small saucepan adding the vinegar, white wine and bouquet garni. Season well and bring to the boil. Cook until the vegetables are tender. Put the salmon into a deep non-metallic dish and pour over the vegetables and liquid. Cover and put in the refrigerator for two days turning the fillets at regular intervals. Take the fillets out of the liquid and place on a serving dish, garnishing with watercress and cucumber. Strain the liquid and serve with the salmon.

Char, a member of the salmon family, is now very rare and caught only in the Lake District. This dish is therefore considered a great delicacy. You can use trout as a cheaper, more readily available alternative.

4 char or trout
1 tsp (5ml) dried dill
2 tsp (10ml) lemon juice
Good pinch of dried nutmeg
Salt and freshly ground black pepper
4 oz (100g) butter, melted

Place the washed fish in a fish kettle and poach gently for about 35-40 minutes, or until the fish is tender. Once the fish is cool enough to handle, remove the skin and bones and flake the flesh into a mixing bowl. Soak the dried dill for 10 minutes in the lemon juice and add to the fish with a generous pinch of ground nutmeg and a good seasoning of salt and black pepper. Mash well (or use a food processor). Pack the fish into individual china pots. Melt the butter and pour through muslin onto the top of each pot to seal. Decorate the tops with a sprig of fresh dill and chill. Serve with lightly buttered brown or granary bread.

Potted Pheasant

Potted pheasant is excellent served as a snack with home baked crusty bread or you could offer it Victorian-style as a special occasion breakfast dish.

1 Cock pheasant, plucked and drawn
Salt and freshly ground black pepper
Good pinch of ground allspice
5 oz (125g) butter
2 tbsp (30ml) sherry
1 tbsp (15ml) lemon juice
3 oz (75g) clarified butter
4 bay leaves

Place the pheasant in a large, heavy-bottomed saucepan, season with salt and black pepper and sprinkle over the allspice. Add 1 oz (25g) of the butter and the sherry, cook over a low heat for about 1½ hours. Remove the pheasant and when cool enough to handle strip off all the meat. Mince the meat very finely into a bowl. Soften the remaining 4 oz (100g) butter and mix with a good seasoning of black pepper and the lemon juice. Pack into small ramekin dishes and spread the tops with clarified butter. Decorate with a bay leaf and chill to seal. Once the seal is broken eat within two days.

Lancashire Hot Pot

N o book on North Country cookery would be complete without this dish which would have been made in times past with mutton and oysters. Mutton is now scarce and oysters expensive so it is now more often made with lamb and mushrooms. It is still a delicious and warming family meal.

3 lbs (1.5kg) best end of lamb, divided into cutlets
1 lb (450g) onions, peeled and sliced
2 carrots, peeled and sliced
4 oz (100g) button mushrooms, whole
Salt and freshly ground black pepper
1 pint (600ml) stock
2 lbs (900g) potatoes, peeled and thickly sliced
1 oz (25g) butter

In a large heavy casserole dish place a layer of cutlets in the base, sprinkle on a layer of onions, scatter some carrot slices on top and some of the mushrooms, seasoning the layer with salt and black pepper. Continue layering the dish. Pour over the stock and then cover with the potato slices, overlapping to seal. Dot with butter, cover tightly and cook for 2½ hours at 180°C, 350°F, gas mark 4, remove the cover and cook for a further 30 minutes.

Shepherds' Pie

It is probable that this dish originates from the Yorkshire Dales and the Cumbrian Fells: the shepherds, after long days and nights tending the sheep, were in need of a substantial and filling meal. It is now popular all over the country but its origins remain in the North where it would only have been made with mutton or lamb.

1 tbsp (15ml) cooking oil
1 onion, finely chopped
1 lb (450g) of lean minced lamb
2 tsp (10ml) flour
½ pint (300ml) beef stock
1 tbsp (15ml) ready-made mint sauce
Salt and freshly ground black pepper
1 lb (450g) cooked and mashed potatoes
1 egg, beaten

Heat the oil in a large frying pan and cook the onion and lamb until browned. Sprinkle over the flour, stir in and cook for a further minute, then add the stock, mint sauce and a good seasoning of salt and black pepper, and bring to the boil, stirring. Transfer the mixture into a large pie dish, leave to cool a little then cover with mashed potato. Brush the potato topping with beaten egg and bake for 45 minutes at 180°C, 350°F, gas mark 4.

Boiled Beef in Ale

Boiling the meat in ale for a long period ensures it is deliciously tender.

3 lbs (1.5kg) brisket or silverside of beef
2 lbs (900g) onions, peeled and sliced
¼ pint (150ml) red wine vinegar
4 oz (100g) black treacle
1 tsp (5ml) ground mace
1 tsp (5ml) turmeric
Bouquet garni
Salt and freshly ground black pepper
1½ pints (900ml) light ale

Place the beef in a large non-metallic dish and scatter over the sliced onions. Mix together the vinegar, treacle, spices and seasoning and pour over the beef. Cover and refrigerate overnight. Transfer the meat, onions and marinade mixture to a large heavy-bottomed saucepan. Pour over the ale and very slowly bring to the boil, add bouquet garni, cover and cook gently on the lowest heat possible for 3-4 hours. Serve sliced with the sauce poured over.

Toad in the Hole

This quick and easy dish of cooked sausages nestling inside a crisp Yorkshire pudding is as popular as ever. The addition of some dried sage to the batter mixture makes it extremely tasty.

4 oz (100g) plain flour
1 tsp (5ml) of dried sage
1 egg
½ pint (300ml) milk
1 oz (25g) melted butter
Pinch of salt
1 lb (450g) pork sausages

Sift the flour and salt into a mixing bowl, make a well in the centre and break in the egg, half the milk and the melted butter, and beat to a smooth batter. Stir in the remaining milk and dried sage. Place the sausages in a small roasting tin and bake in the oven at 220°C, 425°F, gas mark 7 for 10 minutes. Remove from the oven and pour the batter over the sausages. Return to the oven and bake for a further 35-40 minutes.

Omit the sausages, and you have a classic Yorkshire Pudding to accompany a Sunday joint. These quantities will also make six bun-type Yorkshire Puddings in a bun tin (spoon a little fat from the roast into each 'hole' first). Cook at 200°C, 400°F for about 15 minutes or until well-risen and golden brown.

Bread and Butter Pickle

The name of this pickle comes from the old custom of giving children a chunk of bread spread with some beef dripping and topped by a spoonful of pickle to eat on their way to school.

2¼ lbs (1kg) cucumbers
1 lb (450g) onions, peeled and thinly sliced
2 oz (50g) salt
1 pint (600ml) white vinegar
6 oz (170g) sugar
2 tsp (10ml) mustard seeds
½ tsp (2.5ml) ground cloves
1 tsp (5ml) turmeric

Cut the cucumbers into thin slices and put them on a large plate with the onions. Sprinkle with the salt, cover and leave to stand for a few hours. Transfer the cucumber and onion to a colander, drain and rinse well. Place in a large saucepan, add the vinegar, sugar, mustard seeds and spices and heat very gently, stirring from time to time, until the sugar dissolves. Bring to the boil and remove from the heat immediately. Transfer the mixture to warm, sterilised jars. Seal and label, and leave for about six weeks before using.

Steak and Kidney Pie

Originally this rich and tasty pie would have been made with oysters. Today mushrooms are often substituted.

4 oz (100g) butter or margarine, cut into small pieces
2 medium onions, skinned and finely chopped
4 oz (100g) field or wild mushrooms
1 lb (450g) braising steak, trimmed and cubed
8 oz (25g) pig's kidney, trimmed, cored and roughly chopped
1 tbsp (15ml) seasoned flour
¼ pint (150ml) beef stock
¼ pint (150ml) brown ale
1 tbsp (5ml) mixed dried herbs
1 tbsp (15ml) Worcestershire sauce
8 oz (225g) self-raising flour
1 egg, beaten

Melt 1 oz (25g) of butter in a large saucepan and gently fry the onion until soft and transparent. Add the mushrooms and cook for 2 minutes. Add the floured steak and kidney pieces and stir in any remaining seasoned flour. Cook until the meat has browned. Add the stock, ale, herbs and Worcestershire sauce and stir well. Cover and simmer for 1½ hours. Transfer to a pie dish. In a large mixing bowl rub together the self-raising flour, salt and butter with the fingertips. Add sufficient water for a firm but pliable dough. Roll out on a well-floured board and cut a long strip of pastry, dampen the top edge of the pie dish and place the strip all around. Place the remaining pastry on top to form a lid. Brush with beaten egg and bake at 200°C, 400°F, gas mark 6 for 40 minutes.

Meat and Potato Pie

This is one of the most traditional of Northern dishes and reputedly the one most missed by Northerners away from home. The thick pastry lid sets it apart from other pies.

2 onions, peeled and sliced
1 lb (450g) beef skirt, cubed
2 lbs (900g) potatoes, peeled and cubed
Salt and freshly ground black pepper
1 pint (600ml) beef stock
8 oz (225g) self-raising flour
3 oz (75g) margarine
Pinch of salt
1 small egg, beaten

Put the onions, meat and potatoes into a large pie dish, season with salt and black pepper and mix well. Pour over the stock, cover and cook in a low oven at 170°C, 325°F, gas mark 3 for about 2 hours. Put the flour, margarine and a pinch of salt into a mixing bowl. Rub the fat into the flour, using your fingertips, until the mixture resembles fine breadcrumbs. Add sufficient cold water to mix into a firm dough. On a lightly-floured board roll out the pastry to not less than one inch (2.5cm) thickness. Remove the pie from the oven and quickly put on the pastry topping. Brush generously with beaten egg and return to the oven, raising the heat to 200°C, 400°F, gas mark 6 for 30-35 minutes.

Devilled Shoulder or Leg of Lamb

This recipe dates from Georgian times and originates in Yorkshire. There were two methods of "devilling" one dry and one wet. In both methods the meat would be coated in a hot spicy mixture and then grilled or roasted for a dry devil, or cooked in a sauce for a wet devil.

2 tbsp (30ml) seasoned flour
3 lb (1.5kg) shoulder or leg of lamb
1 tbsp (15ml) mild mustard
½ tsp (2.5ml) paprika
¼ tsp (1.2ml) cayenne pepper
½ tsp (2.5ml) turmeric
1 tbsp (15ml) lemon juice
3 oz (75g) softened butter
Salt and freshly ground pepper

Sprinkle a little of the seasoned flour onto the lamb and roast for 30 minutes at 200°C, 400°F, gas mark 6. Meanwhile mix together the mustard, spices, lemon juice, butter and a good seasoning of salt and black pepper in a smooth paste. Remove the lamb from the oven and with a very sharp knife make four or five deep slashes on the fat side, and spoon the devil mixture into the slashes. Sprinkle lightly with some more seasoned flour and return to the oven for a further 30 minutes. Serve with redcurrant or quince jelly.

Pan Haggerty

Originating in Northumberland this economical potato dish is excellent with roast meats.

2 oz (50g) lard or dripping
2 lbs (900g) potatoes, peeled and thinly sliced
1 lb (450g) onions, peeled and thinly sliced
4 oz (100g) Cheddar cheese, grated
Salt and freshly ground black pepper

Melt the lard, or dripping in a large heavy-bottomed frying pan, put a layer of potatoes, then a layer of onions, and then sprinkle some of the grated cheese on top, season with salt and black pepper, and continue layering up the pan finishing with a layer of potatoes. Cook, over a gentle heat, covered (use foil if your frying pan does not have a lid) for about 30 minutes, then invert onto a plate and slide back into the pan to brown the other side for a further 15-20 minutes.

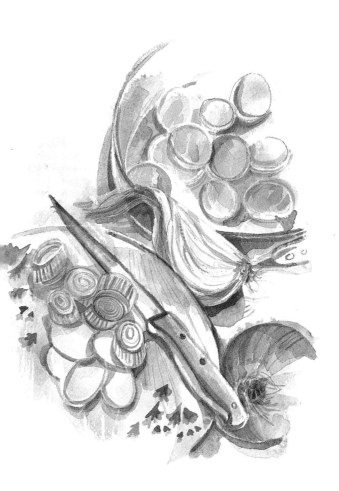

Wensleydale Apple Pie

Apples and cheese have always gone together. Wensleydale was first made in England in the eleventh century by the monks of Jervaulx Abbey in North Yorkshire. After the Abbey was destroyed the local farmers continued to make this distinctive cheese.

4 oz (100g) butter or margarine
8 oz (225g) self-raising plain flour
2 tsp (10ml) caster sugar
3-4 tbsp (45-60ml) milk
1 lb (450g) cooking apples, peeled, cored and sliced
1 oz (25g) sultanas
3 oz (75g) Wensleydale cheese, grated
2 oz (50g) soft brown sugar
1 small egg, beaten

In a mixing bowl rub the fat into the flour with the fingertips until the mixture resembles fine breadcrumbs. Stir in the sugar and add sufficient milk to make a soft dough. Roll out the pastry on a well-floured board and use half to line an 8-inch (20cm) pie or flan dish. Mix the apples, sultanas, grated cheese and brown sugar together and place in the pie dish. Use the remaining pastry for the lid, dampening the edges with water, sealing well and fluting the edges with your fingers. Brush with beaten egg. Make a small slit in the centre of the pie and bake at 200°C, 400°F, gas mark 6 for 35 minutes. Serve hot.

Yorkshire Curd Cheesecake

Cheesecake is one of the earliest known desserts. The Yorkshire version, known as "sweet pye", has a pastry rather than biscuit base and was traditionally eaten by Wolds shepherds to sustain them through sheep shearing. (If you cannot obtain curd cheese use cottage cheese, but it must be sieved).

6 oz (170g) shortcrust pastry
2 oz (50g) caster sugar
1 oz (25g) currants
1 oz (25g) chopped candied peel
2 eggs, beaten
8 oz (225g) curd cheese

Roll out the pastry on a lightly-floured board and use to line an 8-inch flan dish. Cream the butter and sugar together, mix in the currants, candied peel and beaten eggs. Stir in the curds. Pour into the uncooked pastry case and cook for 35-40 minutes in a hot oven at 200°C, 400°F, gas mark 6.

Cumberland Tart

The North Country is very attached to its plate tarts which will be filled with fresh fruits in the summer and dried fruits and syrup in the winter as in this recipe.

12 oz (350g) shortcrust pastry
4 oz (100g) golden syrup
2 oz (25g) butter
5 oz (125g) mixed dried fruit
1 oz (25g) chopped almonds
Good pinch of ground nutmeg
½ tsp (2.5ml) ground mixed spice
1 tbsp (15ml) lemon juice
1 egg, beaten
Sugar for sprinkling

Cut the pastry in half and roll out one half to fit the base of a pie plate. Put the syrup and butter in a saucepan and heat gently until the butter has melted. Mix in the fruits, almonds, spices and lemon juice and spread over the pastry leaving about an inch clear around the outside edge. Brush the edge with water. Roll out the remaining pastry to make a lid, place over the filling, and seal the edges together firmly and decorate. Make a small slit in the centre of the pastry top. Brush the top with beaten egg. Sprinkle over a little caster sugar. Bake in a hot oven at 220°C , 425°F, gas mark 7 for ten minutes then reduce the heat to 180°C, 350°F, gas mark 4 for a further 30-35 minutes. The top should be crunchy. Eat warm with Cumberland Rum Butter.

Newcastle Pudding

This is an old Northumbrian dish dating back to the eighteenth century and is delicious served with lemon sauce.

1 pint (600ml) milk
Grated rind of a lemon
4 oz (100g) glace cherries
6 slices thickly buttered white bread
4 eggs
3 oz (75g) caster sugar
6 oz (170g) granulated sugar
4 tbsp (60ml) water
1 tbsp (15ml) lemon juice
2 tsp (10ml) butter

Heat the milk, without boiling, and add the lemon rind. Remove from the heat and leave to steep for an hour. Butter 1-pint (600ml) pudding basin. Roughly chop the glace cherries and scatter them in the bottom and on the sides of the basin. Fill the basin with the slices of buttered bread (crusts removed). Beat together the eggs and caster sugar until fluffy and then whisk in the milk. Pour over the bread slices. Cover the basin with a double thickness of pleated greaseproof paper (or foil) and steam for two hours.

Sauce: boil the granulated sugar and water for 5 minutes. Remove from heat and beat in butter and the lemon juice. Stir until melted and pour over the pudding.

Victorian Rhubarb Fool

Strangely enough rhubarb originated in Siberia, perhaps that is why it flourishes in the North of England where winters can be extremely cold. Forced rhubarb, whereby the crowns are planted outside but lifted in the autumn and put into "forcing houses", is a thriving business in the North.

1 lb (450g) young rhubarb, trimmed and cut into 1 inch (2.5cm) lengths
2 tbsp (30ml) orange juice
Grated rind of half an orange
3 oz (75g) caster sugar
Pinch mixed spice
½ pint (300ml) double cream
2 tsp (10ml) chopped stem ginger

Put the rhubarb into a saucepan with the orange juice and rind, cover and cook gently for about 15 minutes or until tender. Allow to cool a little. Puree the rhubarb with the sugar and a good pinch of mixed spice in a food processor and allow to cool completely. Whip the cream until really thick and fold into the rhubarb puree. Spoon into glass goblets, chill again. Sprinkle the top with some chopped stem ginger before serving.

Lakeland Damson Cobbler

In the Lyth Valley, just south of Lake Windermere damsons grow in abundance, and this delicious purple black fruit is known locally as the Witherslack damson. is excellent made into jams and jellies, fruit pies, tarts an cobbler - the cobbler being topped with a scone, rathe than pastry lid.

2 lbs (900g) damsons
7 oz (200g) caster sugar
2 oz (50g) butter or margarine
8 oz (225g) self raising flour
Pinch of salt
¼ pint (150ml) milk
1 small egg, beaten

Wash the damsons thoroughly and put into a saucepan with 6oz (170g) of the sugar, add 4 tablespoons of wate and cook over a gentle heat until tender. In a mixing bow rub the fat into the flour and salt using the fingertips unt the mixture resembles fine breadcrumbs. Stir in the rest o the sugar and add sufficient milk to mix to a soft dough Roll out on a lightly-floured board to a ½ inch (1.2cm thickness and using a 2 inch (5cm) cutter cut into rounds Place pitted damsons in a pie dish. Top with overlapping rounds of dough leaving a hole in the centre. Brush wit beaten egg, and bake at 220°C, 425°F, gas mark 7 for abou 15 minutes.

Goosnargh Biscuits

Also known as Goosnargh Cakes, and named after the village in Lancashire where they originated, these distinctively flavoured biscuits are an excellent alternative to shortbread.

6 oz (170g) plain flour
1 tsp (5ml) caraway seeds
½ tsp (2.5ml) ground coriander
4 oz (100g) butter or margarine, cut into small pieces
1 oz (25g) soft light brown sugar
Demerara sugar

Makes about 12

Put the flour, caraway seeds and ground coriander into a mixing bowl, and give a good stir. Rub the fat into the flour using your fingertips until the mixture resembles fine breadcrumbs. Stir in the soft brown sugar, and then knead into a firm smooth dough. On a well-floured board roll out the mixture to about a quarter of an inch thickness (7mm) and using a round cutter, cut into 2 inch (5cm) rounds. Sprinkle a little Demerara sugar on each biscuit, pressing it in gently. Place the biscuits on a lightly-greased baking tray and allow to stand for an hour. Bake at 140°C, 275°F, gas mark 1 for about 35 minutes, or until firm. Cool the biscuits on a wire rack and store in an airtight container.

Singin' Hinny

A well known term of endearment still used today in Northumberland is "Hinny" meaning "Honey", and the "Singin'" comes from the noise that the cake makes as it cooks.

8 oz (225g) self-raising flour
Good pinch of salt
1 oz (25g) butter or margarine
2 oz (50g) lard
2 oz (50g) currants
Single cream

Put the flour and salt in a mixing bowl, cut the butter and lard into small pieces and add to the bowl rubbing the fats into the flour with the fingertips. Stir in the currants and sufficient cream to make a soft dough. Roll out, or press out with your fingers to about one quarter of an inch (7mm) thickness. Prick all over with a fork and either cook on a hot greased griddle for 3-4 minutes each side until golden brown, or bake in the oven at 190°C, 375°F, gas mark 5 for 12-15 minutes. Delicious served hot, split and thickly buttered.

Grasmere Gingerbread

The area around Grasmere in the Lake District is known as Wordsworth country after the famous poet who lived above Rydal Water at Dove Cottage with his sister Dorothy. He was particularly fond of the local gingerbread which you can now buy at the specialist Gingerbread Shop in Grasmere. Alternatively, you can make your own.

8 oz (225ml) plain flour
2 tsp (10ml) ground ginger
4 oz (100g) dark soft brown sugar
¼ tsp (1.2ml) baking powder
4 oz (100g) melted butter

Sift together the flour, ginger and baking powder. Add the melted butter and mix together. Press the mixture evenly, it should be about ½ inch (1cm) thick, into a greased square or oblong tin. Bake at 180°C, 350°F, gas mark 4 for about 35 minutes. Remove from the oven and using a sharp knife cut into squares. Leave to cool in the tin.

Westmoreland Pepper Cake

The addition of pepper to this cake adds an unusual spicy flavour to what would otherwise be a fairly ordinary fruit cake. It is interesting to speculate how the recipe developed but whatever its origin it is a pleasant surprise.

3 oz (75g) raisins
1 oz (25g) currants
1 oz (25g) sultanas
4 oz (100g) caster sugar
3 oz (75g) butter or margarine
8 oz (225g) self-raising flour
½ tsp (2.5ml) ground ginger
½ tsp (2.5ml) ground black pepper
4 tbsp (60ml) milk
2 eggs

Put the fruits, sugar, butter and ¼ pint (150ml) water in a small saucepan and bring to the boil. Lower the heat and simmer for 10 minutes. Remove from heat and leave to cool. Sift the flour, ginger and pepper into a large mixing bowl, and gently stir in the warm fruit mixture, milk and eggs. Turn into a greased and lined 7-8 inch round cake tin and bake for about an hour at 180°C, 350°F, gas mark 4 or until golden and firm to the touch. Turn out and allow to cool on a wire rack.

Cumberland Rum Butter

The origins of Cumberland Rum Butter are believed to be linked with rum smuggling, commonplace along the Cumberland coast in the eighteenth century. The story goes that a broken, smuggled cask hidden in a woman's larder dripped rum onto the butter and sugar stored on the larder shelf. In Cumberland, or Cumbria as it is now known, rum butter is not only eaten with Christmas Pudding, but traditionally served with oatcakes at Christenings.

8 oz (225g) softened, unsalted butter
4 oz (100g) soft light brown sugar
Good pinch of grated nutmeg
1 tbsp (15ml) lemon juice
4 tbsp (60ml) dark rum

Cream the butter, sugar, and nutmeg together until light and fluffy. Beat in the lemon juice and then the rum, a little at a time, beating between each addition, until absorbed into the butter. Pack into an earthenware bowl or dish and serve with any hot steamed pudding.

During the Middle Ages thickened mulled ales achieved great popularity, particularly in the North. Such a drink was considered to give strength after a long cold journey, and one Wharfedale publican was heard to say "it was wonderful if you'd bin drowned".

2 eggs
1 pint (600ml) light ale
1 tbsp (15ml) soft light brown sugar
Pinch of ground nutmeg
1 oz (25g) butter

Serves 2

Beat the eggs with a couple of tablespoons of the ale in a large mixing bowl. Put the rest of the ale into a saucepan and heat gently, but do not allow to boil. When hot pour very carefully over the egg mixture, beating all the time. Return the mixture to the pan, stir in the sugar and a good pinch of ground nutmeg and heat through, but do not allow to boil. Serve in mugs or warmed tankards.

Appletree Press